EXTRATERRESTRIAL LIFE

Alien Encounters

EXTRATERRESTRIAL
LIFE

Alien
Encounters

Patricia D. Netzley

ReferencePoint
Press®

San Diego, CA

© 2012 ReferencePoint Press, Inc.
Printed in the United States

For more information, contact:
ReferencePoint Press, Inc.
PO Box 27779
San Diego, CA 92198
www.ReferencePointPress.com

LIBRARY OF CONGRESS CATALOGING-IN-PUBLICATION DATA

Netzley, Patricia D.
  Alien encounters / by Patricia D. Netzley.
      p. cm. — (Extraterrestrial life series)
  Includes bibliographical references and index.
  ISBN-13: 978-1-60152-169-9 (hardback : alk. paper)
  ISBN-10: 1-60152-169-3 (hardback : alk. paper)
  1. Human-alien encounters—Juvenile literature. 2. Unidentified flying objects—Sightings and encounters—Juvenile literature. 3. Life on other planets—Juvenile literature. I. Title.
  TL789.2.N475 2012
  001.942—dc22
                                                                                    2010053306

CONTENTS

Fiction or Fact?

On the morning of December 1, 1987, retired police officer Philip Spencer headed across a foggy moor in Yorkshire, England, to visit his father-in-law, who lived a 30-minute walk away. Spencer carried a camera so he could take pictures of the moor, but what he captured on film was more exciting than scenery: a humanlike creature less than 4 feet (1.2m) tall with greenish-gray skin.

When Spencer first spotted the creature, it was scrambling over some distant rocks, but after noticing him, it ran away. He gave chase and managed to take a single photograph of it before it disappeared into some brush. Shortly thereafter Spencer saw what looked like a spacecraft rise out of the brush. Before he could take a picture of the craft, it flew away.

Excited, Spencer rushed to a one-hour photo development shop. There he discovered that because his film had been made for taking pictures of

> ## DID YOU KNOW?
>
> According to a report from the Carnegie Institution for Science in Washington, DC, there may be as many as 10 billion trillion planets capable of supporting the creation and continuance of some kind of life.

stationary objects rather than moving ones, his picture of the mysterious being was extremely blurry. Still, he believed his photograph was good enough to convince people he had seen an alien from another planet.

UFO Experts

Spencer contacted a group of ufologists, experts in the study of whether unidentified flying objects (UFOs) might be alien spacecraft. The ufologists examined the image and determined that it had not been created

Philip Spencer's photograph of an alien on a foggy English moor sparked a great deal of interest but the image was too blurry to be viewed as proof of an alien encounter. A computer illustration suggests the scene as it might have looked on that misty morning in 1987.

through clever photographic techniques and was not a picture of any known animal. But they also felt that the image was too blurry for anyone to be sure it depicted an alien.

Believers in extraterrestrials insist that the Ilkley Moor alien photo is among the most convincing evidence that alien spacecraft have visited Earth. In large part this conviction is due to Spencer's reputation for honesty and the fact that he has never tried to profit or achieve fame from his photograph. It is also due to the fact that no one has been able to prove that the Ilkley Moor photo is a fake.

People who believe that humans are the only intelligent beings in the universe, or that at the very least there is no evidence alien spaceships have ever visited Earth, point out that a fake is still a fake even if you cannot prove it is a fake. They also argue that the Ilkley image was undoubtedly created using a model, special effects, and/or photo doctoring. Such critics—referred to in ufology circles as skeptics—also say that if aliens were real, there would be far more photographs of them, along with other types of evidence as well.

Believers Versus Skeptics

But if aliens are not real, why do so many people believe in them? A 2008 poll conducted by the Scripps Howard News Service and Ohio University found that 56 percent of Americans believe that intelligent life probably exists on other planets, and one-third of adult Americans believe that intelligent extraterrestrials have probably already visited Earth. In addition, 1 in 12 Americans have seen a mysterious object in the sky that the observers believe might have carried visitors from another planet.

Skeptics suggest that science-fiction movies and television shows are to blame for such statistics because they make it more likely that certain circumstances or surroundings will trigger thoughts of otherworldly beings. In other words, Spencer imagined he saw an alien and its spaceship simply because the foggy, eerie landscape reminded him of a scene from a science-fiction movie. But believers scoff at skeptics for attributing all reports of alien encounters to mere flights of fancy. Says believer Jim Marrs, "Only those persons whose outlook prevents them from dealing honestly with the massive amount of documentation and reports collected over the past five decades still cling to the idea that nothing soars in the skies of Earth but man's imagination."[1]

Whether one is a believer or a skeptic or something in between, reports of alien encounters promote discussion and controversy. For skeptics, such reports provide opportunities to warn against being too gullible; for believers, they present intriguing possibilities regarding why people might be seeing aliens. In either case, given that hundreds of people claim to have encountered aliens and that many of their stories share common elements, the subject deserves further study.

DID YOU KNOW?

The Committee for Skeptical Inquiry works to discredit claims related to the paranormal, including alien encounters, and publishes one of the leading skeptics' magazines, the *Skeptical Inquirer.*

CHAPTER ONE

Seeing Dead Aliens

In 2007 a sworn affidavit was released to the public concerning events at a military base near Roswell, New Mexico, 60 years earlier. Made by a former public relations officer at the base, Lieutenant Walter Haut, with instructions that it be opened only after his death, the affidavit revealed that Haut helped government officials cover up the existence of two alien bodies at the base. Haut said that these bodies, which he himself saw, had come from a crashed spaceship whose wreckage had fallen on two sites near the base and that the US military cleaned up these sites so that no trace of the crash would remain.

Haut's admissions surprised many ufologists for two reasons. First, while he was stationed at the base, he had worked to convince others that no such spaceship crash had occurred. Second, although in the last years of his life he admitted that he believed the government had covered up the existence of alien bodies, he had never confessed to seeing any himself, even after others made such claims. Consequently, not only skeptics but some believers doubt the truth of his deathbed confessions, while others say that the fact that the confessions were not revealed until after his death—when he could not profit from them—gives them more credibility. Believers also point out that more than 350 people, including medical personnel who were stationed at the base at the time of the

Roswell incident, as it is now commonly known, have also talked about seeing the aliens and/or their spaceship.

The Crash

The Roswell incident began after a thunderstorm on the night of July 2, 1947. The next morning ranch foreman William Ware "Mac" Brazel found an area of debris on the Foster ranch approximately 30 miles (48km) north of Roswell, New Mexico. The debris field was about a quarter mile (0.4km) long and hundreds of feet wide, with a gouge in the ground about 10 feet (3m) wide, 500 feet (152m) long, and 18 inches (46cm) deep, and the debris consisted of hundreds of pieces of what looked like a cross between metal and rubber. Having never seen any material like this and knowing that a military airfield was nearby, Brazel concluded that the debris was a new substance from an experimental craft that had crashed during the thunderstorm.

Brazel took some of the debris to the local sheriff and asked him to call officials at the military base. Shortly thereafter, two intelligence agents showed up to examine the material. One of them, Major Jesse A. Marcel, had never seen this material before so he sent some samples to the military base, and his superiors subsequently sent soldiers to guard the crash site. By this time, rumors were spreading that the debris was from an alien spacecraft that had come down during the storm.

> **DID YOU KNOW?**
>
> Every year during the July 4 weekend, the city of Roswell, New Mexico, hosts the Roswell UFO Festival, an event that brings together people interested in all aspects of alien encounters and includes discussions by leading ufologists.

At first the government seemed to support this position. After the press got word of the crash, officials confirmed to reporters that an alien spaceship had crashed on the Foster ranch and added that the debris had been taken to a military base in Fort Worth, Texas, for further examination. Based on this information, some newspapers published articles saying that the US government now had a "flying saucer" in its possession. But when reporters arrived in Fort Worth to examine pieces of the wreckage, they were told that a mistake had been made; the pieces had come, government agents insisted, from an ordinary weather bal-

General Roger Ramey, commander of the Roswell Army Air Field, identifies metallic fragments found by a New Mexico ranch foreman as pieces of a downed weather balloon. Despite this explanation, many people believe the debris to be from a crashed alien spacecraft.

loon, not a spaceship. To prove this, Marcel—who had accompanied the debris to Fort Worth—held pieces of it up for members of the press to photograph. The resulting images showed material that looked like aluminum foil, effectively ending rumors of an alien crash.

No Weather Balloon

Little more was said about Roswell until Marcel came forward in 1978 to claim that government officials had substituted weather balloon pieces for the real debris. By this time, Marcel had learned that he was dying of cancer, and he did not want to die without revealing what the government had done. He also said that he believed the actual wreckage had indeed come from an alien craft and that the US government had threatened witnesses in order to keep all evidence of extraterrestrials a secret.

Marcel described the crash materials as being made of a substance he had never seen before, surprisingly lightweight and thin but impossible to bend, break, or dent with a hammer. Some of the material reminded him of parchment, yet it would not smoke or burn when a cigarette lighter was held to it. If the material was crinkled up and then released, it would return to its original shape without wrinkles.

In addition, certain pieces, shaped like a steel girder known as an "I" beam but only a few inches long, had strange writing on them. In pink or purplish pink, the writing appeared similar to Egyptian hieroglyphics, although without any animal images, and seemed to have been painted on. However, the "paint" could not be scraped off.

Given all of these strange features, Marcel insisted that the debris was "nothing from the Earth."[2] To ufologists, he was a highly credible witness because he was a military intelligence officer. As former US Air Force

> ### DID YOU KNOW?
>
> In 2007 a farmer in Mexico claimed to have captured and drowned an alien baby on his farm. After studying its corpse, scientists said it was an unknown type of lizard.

captain Kevin D. Randle and ufologist Donald R. Schmitt report in their book *UFO Crash at Roswell*, Marcel "was familiar with all types of aircraft, rockets, balloons, and even the top-secret experiments that were being conducted in New Mexico . . . [yet] he still didn't know what he had seen that day north of Roswell. He went to his grave believing he had held the pieces of spacecraft from another planet."[3]

Alien Bodies

After Marcel came forward to share his opinion, other people began doing the same. Many agreed with Marcel's description of the debris and confirmed that at the time of the Roswell incident, US government agents had threatened to hurt them and their families if they revealed what they knew. Now, though, most felt enough time had passed to make it safe for them to talk.

Some of these witnesses had only seen the debris, either at the crash site or at the Roswell or Fort Worth military bases. Others claimed to have seen alien bodies. Some reported that 4 aliens had been found a short distance away from the Foster ranch crash site—2 dead, 1 dying, and 1 alive but injured—as though they had been thrown from the wreckage. Some witnesses reported that a second spaceship had crashed roughly 150 miles (241km) west of the Foster ranch near Socorro, New Mexico, and that this site had 4 alien bodies, 1 possibly alive. Still other people said that there was a third crash site with 5 alien corpses, although these witnesses said that no corpses had been found at the Foster ranch site. In the affidavit produced in 2007, Haut insisted that there were 2 crash sites and said that 2 bodies were found at the second site.

Witness descriptions of these aliens also varied. The extraterrestrials were anywhere from 3 feet 6 inches (107cm) to 5 feet 3 inches (160cm) in height, and their eyes were either smaller or larger than human eyes. Most witnesses agree, however, that the aliens' heads were unusually large, with small noses and ears, and that they had leathery, hairless, gray skin.

Some people, like Haut, did not see the aliens' clothing because their bodies were covered with a tarp, but others reported that the aliens wore

Alien Cemetery

Sometimes while excavating ancient sites, scientists discover remains that appear to be extraterrestrial. For example, in the late 1930s dozens of 4-foot-tall bodies (122cm) with unusually large heads were discovered in caves along the Tibet-China border, and in 2009 Swiss anthropologist Hugo Children announced the discovery of a cemetery in central Africa holding over 200 7-foot-tall bodies (213cm) with unusually large heads. The anthropologist theorized that these were aliens killed by a virus after establishing a colony on Earth. However, he refused to reveal the location of the site, saying he wanted to protect it from outsiders until further studies could be done. Skeptics say this secrecy suggests the site does not exist, but if it does, they argue, then the bodies and all similar ones are nothing more than the remains of humans with genetic abnormalities.

silver-gray jumpsuits with no buttons, snaps, or zippers. Some saw the aliens on gurneys, some on the ground. Some said the beings appeared to have been bandaged. A few witnesses said the dead aliens smelled odd, perhaps from a preservative known as formaldehyde, and a mortician near the military facility said he had received a phone call from someone there asking how to preserve alien bodies.

Both a nurse and a pathologist who had worked at the military hospital stated they had personally examined the dead aliens, and several military officers insisted they saw the pathologist's report, which included photographs of the aliens. A photographer claimed to have taken pictures of the aliens when they were lying dead on tarps near the Foster crash site and of the wreckage as well. A soldier who had guarded the Foster crash site also claimed to have seen the dead aliens, as did a soldier who escorted the bodies to the hospital; the escort believed that one of the aliens had been alive. A secretary at the air field, Norma Gardner, said she typed reports on autopsies of the aliens and saw the bodies once they had been preserved in a chemical solution.

Government Threats

These and many other witnesses also provided details about threats they had received from government agents. The mortician, for example, said that a captain from the base told him that if he did not keep quiet, he would be killed and his body dumped in the desert. A firefighter who saw one of the crash sites reported hearing the same threat. Relatives of the sheriff to whom Brazel had first reported his discovery said that military police had threatened to kill their entire family if even one of them kept talking about the incident.

Brazel himself was also apparently threatened shortly after he discovered the debris. He was taken into military custody and held at the military base for several days, after which he stopped saying the debris had come from anything but a weather balloon. From then on, Brazel expressed dislike for the military. Several reporters also said they had been intimidated into promoting the weather balloon story, or at least not repeating anything they had heard related to aliens.

Someone who backed up claims of government intimidation was Brigadier General Arthur E. Exon, who had been a lieutenant colonel at Wright-Patterson Air Force Base in Dayton, Ohio, during the Roswell incident. Records indicate that whatever was found in Roswell, at least some of it was transported from Fort Worth to the intelligence center at Wright-Patterson. Exon said he was certain the bodies were still being stored there, although he never saw them himself, and said he knew people who had tested the spacecraft debris. He also said that to keep the existence of the aliens from the public, the government had created a secret military group dedicated to squelching Roswell alien stories and controlling access to all information related to the crash.

DID YOU KNOW?

In 2009 an American TV crew found what appeared to be a mummified alien in northern Chile. However, the crew was not allowed to remove the mummy for study, and skeptics suggest it was a fake planted by locals wanting to increase tourism.

In his affidavit Haut said that he saw the spacecraft in a hanger at the base. Prior to this confession—before he admitted having seen the bodies and craft himself—he stated that he believed the government was hiding evidence of the crash, telling ufologists Randle and Schmitt, "I think there was one gigantic cover-up on this thing. I think somewhere all this material is stashed away."[4] In *UFO Crash at Roswell*, Randle and Schmitt say that government records on Roswell support this. They note that when records on the Roswell incident were released to the public in 1976, the file contained only a press clipping. "No letters, no notes, no investigative forms, no official weather balloon explanation, nothing but that lone clipping," they report. "The file for the recovery of an actual weather balloon in Circleville, Ohio, a week before the Roswell event contains far more documentation on its particulars. Where is the material that should be in the Roswell file?"[5]

Autopsy Hoax

By the mid-1990s popular books detailing witness accounts of the Roswell aliens convinced many Americans that the government was hiding evidence of contact with extraterrestrials. Also influential was a film offered by video producer Ray Santilli in 1995. It contained supposedly genuine, unedited black-and-white historical footage from what Santilli said was a Roswell alien autopsy. Later that year, the Fox television network twice aired a documentary on the footage, *Alien Autopsy: Fact or Fiction?*, that seemed to support Santilli's claims. This program was ultimately viewed by millions of people in over 30 countries.

However, in 2006 Santilli admitted that his footage was not real but a reconstruction. He said that he had seen the real footage several years earlier but that all but a few frames had been damaged and then lost before he could buy it from the owner. Therefore, he had re-created the footage himself, using dummies and props, and incorporated the few authentic frames into his film. (Santilli has never said which frames in his footage are "original.")

Dead Humans?

Even before Santilli's confession, though, some people were publicly doubting his film's authenticity, and the air force released reports that indicated the Roswell debris had come from a top-secret military project involving high-altitude balloons that acted like spy satellites, carrying devices to detect nuclear missiles and missile tests in foreign countries. The aliens seen by witnesses, the air force said, were either dummies used in testing various experimental craft or injured or dead pilots of such craft.

Indeed, photographs of other "alien autopsies" have clearly shown human victims instead of alien ones. In one such case, although the pilot was badly mangled, he could still be identified as human by the cast-off glasses visible in the photo. And records from the Roswell air field suggest that one crash involving human pilots had circumstances strikingly similar to those associated with its supposed alien autopsies. Skeptic and amateur astronomer Timothy Printy reports that on June 26, 1956, a plane filled with fuel crashed a few miles south of the base and its crew burned to death. He says that autopsies had to be performed on the deceased to determine each one's identity, and that "the descriptions of the bodies in the autopsy reports closely match"[6] descriptions of the condition of the aliens' bodies.

Printy therefore believes that witnesses to the Roswell incident, who were recounting events that had happened decades earlier, were actually incorporating memories of the plane crash and its victims into their stories about the Roswell incident. But believers counter that given the many credible witnesses associated with the Roswell incident, the type of confusion that Printy is talking about is highly unlikely. They also insist that dozens of other spaceship crashes have occurred in places that have never been associated with human autopsies.

Other Roswells

According to ufologists, some of these other crashes have been in foreign countries, including Brazil, Canada, Norway, and South Africa. One 1969 crash in Russia was associated with alien-autopsy footage similar to the Roswell footage promoted by Santilli, but even some ufologists say this footage is probably a hoax. However, ufologists do think that alien bodies have been discovered in other countries as well as in the United States. They estimate that the number of alien bodies retrieved from crash sites worldwide is over 130 and that more than a dozen aliens have been taken alive.

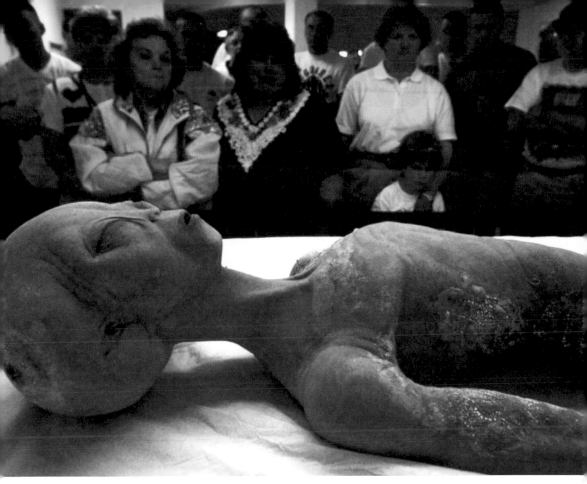

Reports of alien bodies being carried from a 1947 crash site near Roswell, New Mexico, have circulated widely over the years. This alien replica matches descriptions given at the time: it has a large head, small nose and ears, and leathery, hairless gray skin.

One example of a foreign case similar to Roswell supposedly took place in Mexico on the night of August 25, 1974. This incident began with US defense radar detecting a UFO approaching the United States from the Gulf of Mexico at a speed of roughly 2,500 miles per hour (4,000kph). The UFO did not remain at this speed or course, however; it slowed down, decreased altitude twice (leveling off in between each descent), and made a turn before finally disappearing from radar near Coyame, a town in the state of Chihuahua, Mexico. Less than an hour later, a commercial airplane en route from El Paso, Texas, to Mexico City crashed in the same area.

Alien Technology

In his 1997 book, *The Day After Roswell*, former army intelligence colonel Philip Corso claims to have seen the body of a dead alien while stationed at Fort Riley in Kansas in 1947. The alien, he said, was in a glass box suspended in a blue liquid, and it was roughly 4 feet (122cm) tall, with a large, lightbulb-shaped head and only 4 fingers on each hand. Corso also claims that in 1961 he read secret government documents, including an alien-autopsy report, revealing that the bodies of the Roswell aliens were sent to Walter Reed Hospital in Washington, DC, shortly after the crash. In addition, according to Corso, parts of the Roswell spacecraft were sent to various defense companies for study, and the aliens' technology led to the creation of such important earthly technologies as integrated circuitry, fiber optics, night vision equipment, and the laser. Corso believes that the US government covered up the true nature of the crash not only to keep the American public from knowing about the extraterrestrials' visit but to keep foreign governments from knowing about the new technologies the aliens brought to Earth.

The next day an air search for the lost plane spotted two sites of wreckage on the ground a few miles apart. Radioing this information to authorities, someone on the search plane said that one of the sites contained an odd craft, seemingly undamaged but saucer shaped. After this, Mexican authorities ordered radio silence on the matter. Nonetheless, according to people claiming to have been involved in the Chihuahua incident, the Central Intelligence Agency (CIA) had already intercepted the first transmissions on the matter and sent a spaceship recovery team to nearby Fort Bliss, across the border in Texas. This team, informants say, included several unmarked helicopters whose pilots intended to fly them into Mexico undetected.

Meanwhile, Mexican authorities had apparently loaded the alien craft onto a flatbed truck as part of a military convoy transporting it and the airplane wreckage elsewhere—but the convoy never reached its destination. Informants claim that US satellite images showed the vehicles stopped on a remote road, their doors open and two human bodies near-by. When CIA helicopters flew to the site, the recovery team discovered the rest of the people involved in the convoy dead inside their trucks.

Ufologists say that the CIA burned the dead and blew up the abandoned vehicles after removing the spaceship from the flatbed truck and putting it into a large transport helicopter. The alien craft—said to be silver, windowless, unmarked, and just over 16 feet (4.9m) in diameter—was then supposedly taken to Wright-Patterson or perhaps a more secret military base. Some people insist that alien bodies were taken there too, although no one can agree on how many bodies there were.

Storytelling

Skeptics say that such disagreements are proof that reports of alien crashes are products of imagination. In fact, conflicting details cause even some ufologists to question the nature of alien-encounter stories. In his book, *The Myth and Mystery of UFOs*, ufologist Thomas E. Bullard notes that many aspects of the Roswell story, including the number of crash sites and key details related to the bodies and objects found at those sites, have changed over the years. Moreover, he says, "the Roswell mythology continues to flourish and evolve as claimants continue to come forward with accounts of seeing wreckage or working with unearthly technology."[7]

Others have also equated the Roswell incident with mythology or folklore. For example, in their book, *UFO Crash at Roswell: The Genesis of a Modern Myth*, Benson Saler, Charles A. Ziegler, and Charles B. Moore say that the only way to understand Roswell is by looking at it as an example of mythology. According to a review of the book by the National Library of Australia, the authors believe that the Roswell story is "similar to traditional myths in transmission, structure, and motif," and "taps into modern beliefs in the power of technology and the duplicity of a monolithic government."[8] Others have compared aliens to creatures from folklore, such as elves and goblins, while government agencies represent evil empires or kingdoms that seek to suppress the truth.

In his book *The Skeptic's Dictionary*, skeptic Robert T. Carroll takes a harsher view of the Roswell story, referring to elements of it as "delusions."[9] These delusions, he says, came together to create a fanciful tale that many people believe in as deeply as they might a religion. In speaking of how this tale was formed, he explains: "An extraordinary story is told, then retold with embellishments and re-modeled with favorable points emphasized while unfavorable ones are dropped. False witnesses put in their two cents. . . . [This created a] mountain of falsehoods that became part of the UFO memory, fixating conviction in a remarkable tale."[10]

Physical Damage

Believers, of course, do not view themselves as mythmakers or the equivalent of religious fanatics. They also say that positions like Carroll's ignore the fact that the ground at a crash site often shows signs that something big impacted with it. In Roswell, for example, there were large gouges in the ground, and other sites have displayed similar gouges and/or broken foliage. In fact, approximately 20 percent of UFO reports are accompanied by physical traces that suggest a spaceship landing or crash. These might include not only plant and/or soil damage and metal debris but the destruction of nearby objects. For example, after a January 2009 incident in northern England, the blade of a wind turbine was destroyed by what many people believe was an alien spacecraft. "I actually saw a white light—a round, white light that seemed to be hovering"[11] over the turbine before the blade sheared off, a local politician said afterward.

> **DID YOU KNOW?**
>
> Alien autopsies have been re-created at least 14 times for movies, TV shows, or magazine photo shoots or by people just wanting to prove they can make such an autopsy look real on film.

In this case witnesses say the UFO did not crash but instead flew away, leaving believers and skeptics to argue over what might have caused the damage. Such arguments are a feature of all cases where the appearance of a UFO has supposedly left physical traces behind. Scientific tests on soil, foliage, and debris have so far been inconclusive as to whether these things came into contact with something extraterrestrial, while witness statements about alien bodies have largely been ignored by the scientific community.

CHAPTER TWO

Seeing Live Aliens

In January 2007 in Fayetteville, North Carolina, a group of 5 men fishing on the banks of the Cape Fear River spotted 3 UFOs in the sky. Afraid these were alien spacecraft, they abandoned their fishing gear, jumped in their cars, and raced away. Once home, one of the men, Chris Bledsoe Sr., saw a strange being in some nearby woods; it was 3 feet (91cm) tall and had red eyes, and its skin looked as though it had been coated with glass. Meanwhile, another of the men, Chris Bledsoe Jr., saw several similar figures emerge from the woods near his house. Though the 2 men were well-respected in their town, they hesitated to tell other people what they had experienced. Once they told their story they encountered disbelief even from those closest to them.

Similarly, one night in October 1973, 26-year-old police chief Jeff Greenhaw of Falkville, Alabama, went to investigate a report of a UFO and spotted a figure by the side of the road. "It was real bright," he later said, "something like rubbing mercury on nickel, but just as smooth as glass—different angles giving different lighting."[12] Greenhaw took some pictures of the creature, which wore an odd, silver suit and had an antenna on its head, before it sprinted away. He noted that it "seemed to have springs in the feet for propulsion" that enabled it to "run faster than any human."[13] The next day, when Greenhaw told other people in town what he had seen, they ridiculed him. When he showed them his photographs, they insisted the images were of a man either wrapped in aluminum foil or wearing an asbestos suit. Branded a liar, Greenhaw lost his job, and shortly thereafter his marriage ended in divorce.

The Flatwoods Monster

The ridicule experienced by Greenhaw and others reporting alien encounters is common, even when several people claim to have seen the same thing. In cases of multiple reports, if the witnesses are credible and not obvious pranksters, skeptics say the people involved are all experiencing mass hysteria. That is, after hearing about an alien sighting, others panic and think they have seen an alien too, perhaps imagining that some ordinary creature is actually a monster.

For example, in 2000 skeptic Joe Nickell of what was then called the Committee for the Scientific Investigation of Claims of the Paranormal

Jeff Greenhaw's black and white photos (pictured), taken at night on an Alabama road in 1973, reveal bizarre images of what appears to be an extraterrestrial being in a silver suit. Greenhaw was ridiculed by those who heard his story and saw the photographs.

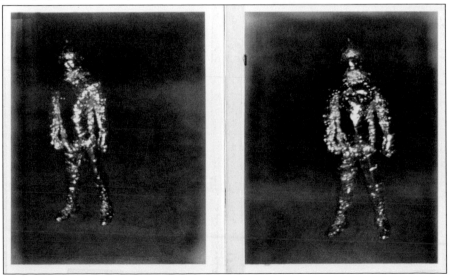

(now known as the Committee for Skeptical Inquiry), conducting investigations into old cases of alien encounters, declared that sightings of the Flatwoods Monster years earlier had actually been an encounter with an owl. These sightings took place in Braxton County, West Virginia, in September 1952, after a ball of fiery light streaked across the night sky and came down on a rise within wooded farmland. Witnesses said the ball turned and slowed down before landing rather than crashing to the ground. Nonetheless, at the time, government officials insisted it was a meteor, and Nickell agrees with this assessment.

People who actually saw the ball, however, believed it to be something mysterious, and several of them headed into the woods with flashlights to investigate. This group was made up of five children, the mother of two of the children, and National Guardsman Eugene Lemon. Lemon's dog was out ahead of them, and as the group approached the landing site, the dog ran away from it, clearly terrified. Still, they pressed on, and as they approached the rise, they smelled a foul odor and noticed an odd mist along the ground that made them cough and gag.

Within the mist was an egg-shaped red object that might have been a spacecraft, and alongside it was a 10-foot-tall humanoid creature (305cm) with a spade-shaped head and glowing red eyes. It hissed loudly and started toward the group, then changed course to head back toward the object. As soon as it turned away, the people fled.

One of them then alerted authorities about the strange creature, but although the local sheriff and a reporter subsequently encountered the noxious mist, they saw neither the spacecraft nor the creature. However, while continuing their investigation the next morning, they discovered gouges in the ground and scorch marks on nearby trees. Witnesses later suggested that perhaps the wood was burned by rays coming out of the creature's glowing red eyes.

Multiple Witnesses

By this time, more people had seen the creature than just the group in the woods. Apparently the Flatwoods Monster had wandered through the area before disappearing. These additional sightings, ufologists say, lent credibility to the initial sighting. As William J. Birnes explains in his book *Aliens in America*:

> The multiple witness testimony of the creature's appearance was . . . convincing because of the consistency of the stories and the descriptions. Some skeptics argue that the first group of witnesses . . . actually saw a barn owl in the woods and then panicked. These arguments . . . don't pan out . . . because there were too many different sightings of the creature in too many different places. Certainly, if the only people to have seen the monster were the first group of witnesses, then the story would have less credibility. But other witnesses would come across the creature in other areas, and added to trace evidence of burn marks on the trees, the consistency of the accounts lends more credence to the story.[14]

The US government's involvement in this incident also made witness reports more credible. The military cordoned off the area shortly after the spacecraft sighting was reported, an action that was not typical at that time for a meteor crash. In addition, military fighter jets had been spotted flying over the area right before the incident, leading some people to suspect that the craft of the Flatwoods Monster had landed to avoid being shot down.

The Appearance of Mothman

Despite the credible aspects of this incident, Birnes admits that it is "one of the more incredible stories coming out of the 1950s UFO phenomenon."[15] For this reason, he thinks it would have been dismissed as just another unbelievable tale had it not been for the appearance of a similarly strange creature known as the Mothman. First sighted in the Pleasant Point area of West Virginia in November 1966 but also seen in other places in the decades since then, this creature is said to have glowing eyes much like those of the Flatwoods Monster and to emit a high-pitched squeal when encountered.

However, the Mothman also has wings, is not quite as tall as the Flatwoods Monster—7 feet (213cm) as opposed to 10 feet (305cm)—and has never been seen with a spacecraft. Moreover, Mothman reports tend to occur right before a deadly disaster. This, plus the creature's wings, have led some people to call it a fallen angel much like Satan. Others have suggested it is an earthly paranormal being in the same category as Bigfoot or the Loch Ness Monster.

The majority of those who believe in Mothman, however, insist it is an extraterrestrial, perhaps with the ability to travel through time to witness Earth's disasters. As Birnes notes: "When you put the Flatwoods Monster and the Mothman together . . . you might ask whether human beings share this planet with a more diverse group of creatures than we realize. Some may be from here, but how many are from other worlds?"[16]

Lizardmen

In addition to one-of-a-kind creatures like the Flatwoods Monster and the Mothman, some people report having seen groups of monster-like aliens that look similar to one another. Among these are the Reptilians. Also known as the Reptiloids or the Reptoids, they are lizard-like beings that British author David Icke has theorized come from the Alpha Draconis star system. (His supporters therefore call the beings Draconians.) Icke has suggested that these aliens are interdimensional as well as extraterrestrial, meaning they can travel from dimension to dimension as well as from planet to planet. Some witnesses, such as police officer Herbert Schirmer of Ashland, Nebraska, in 1967, have reported seeing Reptiloids with their spaceship. Others have encountered them near or inside caves and tunnels, leading some people to believe that these aliens have underground bases on Earth.

A typical example of a cave sighting is that of two children in the Nevada Desert in 1977. Writing in 2010 about the boys' experience, their mother, Cherry Hinkle, tells of her sons, Harry and Marc, finding a strange underground room within Black Mountain near Henderson, Nevada. In a tunnel beyond this room, they found a strangely engraved metal rod beside a closed metal door. After they picked up the rod, the door began to open and the boys ran. Once outside, they heard a growl, and according to Hinkle: "Harry and Marc looked back at the cave entrance and . . . [saw] a very large greenish humanoid . . . [forcing] his big body out of the narrow cave. The boys screamed and started running down the slope of the hill."[17]

Accounts of alien sightings in the woods of West Virginia in the 1950s described an unusually tall humanoid being with a spade-shaped head and glowing red eyes. It might have looked something like the creature depicted in this computer illustration.

Aliens Attracted to Water

Some UFO sightings suggest that the aliens might have an interest in Earth's water. For example, in June 1977 a man in the Dominican Republic spotted a disc-shaped spacecraft hovering over the ocean, using a long tube apparently to suck up water. The witness saw aliens inside the spacecraft, peering through windows at the tube. In March 1978 off the coast of Guaiuba, Brazil, a man saw a similar craft putting a tube into the ocean, but in this case 2 3-foot-tall (91cm) aliens came out of the craft to manipulate the tube. More recently, in March 2001, 2 men saw a disc-shaped UFO hovering over Brazil's River Tocantins, and standing on its outer hull was a 4-foot-tall (122cm) alien dangling a hose into the water. In many cases witnesses describe the tube as being attached to a mechanical device or box rather than directly to the ship. Some ufologists believe that the aliens are taking water samples, while others suggest that the aliens are replenishing their own water supply on the ship. Still others suggest that instead of pumping water into the ship, the aliens might be pumping waste matter out of the ship and into the water.

Hinkle says that when they got home the boys were hysterical and claimed the lizardman had followed them to their door, but she saw nothing outside her front window. However, that night at around 2 A.M., she was awakened by a noise, looked out the window again, and saw the creature for herself. Over 7 feet tall (213cm), it had a large head, pointed teeth, and golden eyes, and it was attempting to open her window with the claws on its webbed hands. Eventually, it gave up and left, but Hinkle decided it was after the metal rod her sons had brought home. The next day she placed the rod just outside the cave and never saw the lizardman again.

Little Green Men

Similar to the lizardmen are the little green men. Throughout the first half of the twentieth century, most aliens in fiction were described as small, green humanoids, and beginning in 1908, newspapers sometimes reported on supposedly real sightings of these creatures. Consequently, by the 1950s the phrase "little green men" had become synonymous with "extraterrestrials." However, the phrase became especially popular after news reports in 1955 about little green men attacking people in Indiana and Kentucky.

The first attack occurred in Evansville, Indiana, on August 14, 1955, when a woman swimming in the Ohio River, Mrs. Darwin Johnson, was nearly drowned by something in the water. She later said it had human-like arms and hands but also claws and fur. Her swimming companions rescued her from the creature, which disappeared beneath the water as they fled the river. They then reported their experience to law enforcement and the press, saying they had seen UFOs overhead while fleeing, but authorities found no evidence to support their story.

A few days later, on the night of August 21, 1955, 11 members of 2 families, the Suttons and the Calloways, encountered a similar being. They were staying in the Suttons' farmhouse near the towns of Kelly and Hopkinsville in Kentucky when one of them saw a UFO while getting water from an outdoor pump. After he told the others what he had seen, they insisted it must have been a shooting star. An hour later they all heard noises outside. According to what the witnesses said later, 2 of the men grabbed guns, went out on the porch to check on the noises, and discovered a humanoid several feet away. (In subsequent news reports the number of humanoids grew to 15 or 20, and they were supposedly next to a spaceship.)

An Alien Attack?

About 4 feet (122cm) tall, the humanoid was dressed in what appeared to be metallic clothing and had green skin, a big head, pointed ears, and clawed hands. Some of the witnesses later said its clothing glowed; others said its eyes glowed. In either case when the creature rushed toward the two men they started shooting at it. It jumped onto the roof of the farmhouse, seemingly wounded, and tried to grab them as they stepped off the porch. They fired their guns at it again until it jumped down from the roof and ran off.

The two men then went back inside the house to tell the others what had happened. A few minutes later a creature appeared at the window, and one of the men shot at it through the glass. It darted away, and soon there were noises on the roof. Shortly thereafter, witnesses saw a creature peeking in the window but could not tell whether it was the same creature or a different one. Before they could shoot at it, it ran away. For the next few hours, the noises and window peeks continued, with seven of the witnesses seeing the creatures, although no one could agree on just how many might be outside. By this time, a highway patrol officer had reported seeing several UFOs in nearby skies.

Finally, during a lull in the activity, the two families managed to dash out of the farmhouse and into their cars. They then headed directly to the police station in Hopkinsville. Nearly two dozen police officers immediately rushed to the farmhouse, but they found no sign of any creatures. They did, however, find a strange glowing substance on a fence as well as evidence of a gun battle.

The police also found the witnesses to be credible. When interviewed separately they told consistent stories and they were clearly shaken up by whatever had happened on the farm. In addition, when Johnson saw a witness sketch of the Kelly-Hopkinsville creature, she insisted that it looked like whatever had attacked her in the Ohio River.

However, people who lived near the Sutton farmhouse said that although they did hear gunshots coming from the farm, they did not hear anywhere near the number of shots the witnesses claimed had been fired. Moreover, the damage to the shot window suggested that a pistol had been used rather than the reported shotgun. These discrepancies between

> ## DID YOU KNOW?
>
> Media accounts in 1938 of the panic caused by Orson Wells's Halloween radio version of a fictional story, *The War of the Worlds* by H.G. Wells, said that people who thought the broadcast was a real news report about an alien invasion were convinced "little green men" were going to kill them.

the evidence and the story led the press to speculate that the two families were perpetrating a hoax, while those who considered them honest thought they were victims of a prank. Still others have suggested that the creatures might have been ordinary animals—perhaps monkeys escaped from a circus—which mass hysteria turned into "aliens." Many ufologists, however, consider the Hopkinsville case to be an example of a real alien encounter despite any discrepancies in witness accounts.

The Nordics

Not all alien encounters, though, involve creatures that look like goblins, reptiles, or monsters. Some feature aliens that resemble humans from Scandinavia. Known as the Nordics, these extraterrestrials are said to have blond hair, blue eyes, and pale skin and are anywhere from 6 to 8 feet (183cm to 244cm) tall. They are also said to have the ability to communicate with humans telepathically, mind to mind. Ufologist Donald Worley, who specializes in studying reports of Nordics, says that most of the Nordics seen by humans are male adults and that they wear either "skin-tight suits or flowing white robes."[18]

Worley also says that after studying 50 cases of Nordic encounters in depth, out of a total of 150 encounters in all, he has found that Nordics are friendly and that their telepathic communications can leave humans in a state of euphoria or with feelings of love. Consequently, some of the people who have encountered Nordics compare them to angels. Others, however, disagree with this assessment. For example, one of Worley's research subjects, a woman from New Hampshire named Michelle, says: "They are not Gods or angels. They are another race who are here because they are responsible for us."[19]

> **DID YOU KNOW?**
>
> Italian paintings created around 10,000 BC and a Mayan stone carving on a sarcophagus from the AD 600s show a figure that appears to be an astronaut; some people believe this proves extraterrestrials have been visiting Earth since ancient times.

Other people claiming to have seen Nordics have also called them caretakers of Earth and its humans. Some of these people believe that the Nordics want to help humans move into a new plane of existence. A few also believe that the Nordics are somehow related to humans, and that perhaps the Nordics once lived on Earth but abandoned it for another planet. There are also those who believe the Nordics are only pretending to help humans but are in fact evil beings who perhaps already have armed spaceships heading to Earth from some distant planet. But good or evil, the Nordics are typically said to be the enemies of another type of alien, the Greys.

The Greys

The Greys are the most commonly reported type of extraterrestrial in modern times. In fact, 50 percent of all alien reports in the United States and Australia and 90 percent of all alien reports in Canada involve Greys. They are also the aliens typically featured in alien-autopsy stories and films, including those associated with the Roswell incident.

Named for their gray or grayish-white skin, the Greys are typically described as hairless humanoids with unusually large heads and large, almond-shaped eyes. These aliens are also said to have slender bodies, short legs, and long, thin arms and fingers. Reports differ as to whether they have mouths or nostrils, but if they do, these are typically described as being tiny slits, as are their ears. Most witnesses also say that the Greys communicate telepathically.

As for the Greys' height, witnesses typically place these aliens into two categories. One type of Grey is from 2 to 4 feet (61cm to 122cm)

> ### DID YOU KNOW?
>
> Some ufologists believe that an ancient Peruvian people known as the Nazca created a landing strip for alien spaceships sometime between 400 BC and AD 900. This area is marked with drawings that can only be seen in their entirety from a point miles above Earth.

Lightning illuminates Nevada's Black Mountain—the site of a 1977 alien encounter in which two boys supposedly saw a large, greenish, lizard-like humanoid squeezing out of a narrow cave. The mother of the boys later reported seeing the same creature outside their home.

tall, while the other is around 5 feet (152cm) tall. The smaller Greys are said to have smooth skin similar to a dolphin's, whereas the skin of the taller Greys appears rough and leathery. The taller ones, who seem to be in charge, sometimes wear a coat similar to what a doctor or scientist might wear. They also appear to work individually, whereas the smaller aliens typically work in groups. Some witnesses also report that the taller aliens look like individuals—that is, witnesses could tell them apart—whercas the smaller aliens all look exactly alike.

Witness disagreements about the nature of the aliens' eyes have also led some to wonder whether the beings are capable of altering

The Pine Bush Vortex

From the beginning of the twentieth century, people in the town of Pine Bush, New York, have spotted UFOs in the form of glowing, floating balls of light. By the 1980s these sightings had become so numerous that sometimes there would be more than a dozen in a single night. Some residents claimed to have seen alien spacecraft in addition to the balls of light. In the 1990s some people claimed to have seen mysterious beings and creatures as well, and sometimes residents heard strange rumblings coming from deep beneath the ground. After studying the geology and magnetic fields in these areas, geologist Bruce Cornet concluded that devices buried deep within Earth, perhaps within an underground base, were transmitting photon beams up through the ground and into outer space. In 2000 he suggested that Pine Bush might be the site of an energy vortex that made it possible for aliens to travel from one dimension or world to another. By this time, Cornet was claiming to have seen aliens and to have communicated with them telepathically. He also produced a videotape in 1997 of a flying black triangle that he said was an alien spacecraft.

their appearance. Jim Moroney, who claims to have encountered some Greys in 1987, discusses this possibility in his book *The Extraterrestrial Answer Book*. He notes that while many witnesses insist the aliens have black, lifeless eyes with no pupils, irises, corneas, or eyelids, he saw blue eyes that were humanlike, though still quite large. Consequently, Moroney says:

> I believe that the blue eyes were their attempt to soften my experience with them. Whether they had actually made alterations to their physical appearance or had simply altered [through telepathy] the way I perceived them, they made sure that I saw what I needed to see [in order to stay calm]. This sort of behavior would go a long way toward explaining why a variety of . . . appearances have been described for the aliens, the small-statured, large-headed beings being only one of them.[20]

In other words, maybe the reason people have seen so many different kinds of aliens—Greys, Nordics, little green men, monsters—is because the aliens can appear less threatening if they want to.

Media Influences?

Skeptics, however, insist that people's descriptions of aliens are based on experiences with popular media. In this view, the reason more people report seeing Greys as opposed to other types of aliens is because far more aliens in fiction look like the Greys. Skeptic Aaron Sakulich says:

> In the 30s and 40s, the little gray men were the solid foundation of such comic books as Amazing Stories, Wonder Stories, and Science Wonder Stories. Unless you were living in a cave, you couldn't turn around without bumping into a representation of big-headed little gray men. The simple fact is that they've been a part of popular culture, an especially well-recognized part of popular culture, since the 1890s.[21]

Indeed, the first mention of a being with a large head and weak body appeared in 1893 in an article by H.G. Wells, "The Man of the Year Million," in which he theorized that humans of the future would have these features because of their sedentary lives. Wells also used this description for the aliens in his 1901 novel, *The First Men in the Moon*. By this time, newspapers had published drawings of big-headed, skinny-bodied aliens. In the decades since then, Grey-like aliens have appeared in countless stories, novels, TV shows, movies, and video games. Consequently, Sakulich asserts that "the sighting of little gray

> ### DID YOU KNOW?
>
> In the 1950s author George Adamski became famous for his claims that aliens from Venus had been visiting him to promote peace and warn people about an impending nuclear war.

space aliens is the product of more than a hundred years of seeing their form in culture. End of story."[22]

But is that the end of the story? What about cases where people report not just having seen aliens but having been taken into their spaceships? How did the first stories of alien abduction come about, and why are they so consistent with one another? Skeptics blame the media for this as well, while believers say that these alien encounters are far too complex for people like Sakulich to dismiss as the result of "a combination of pop culture and being crazy."[23]

CHAPTER THREE

Abducted by Aliens

O n October 10, 1973, more than a dozen people, including two police officers, reported seeing a silver, slow-moving UFO over New
Orleans, Louisiana. The next night, two men less than 200 miles (322km)
away in nearby Pascagoula, Mississippi, saw something similar. Charlie
Hickson, age 42, and Calvin Parker, age 19, later reported that they had
been fishing off a pier on the Pascagoula River when they heard a buzzing
or whirring sound, similar to an electric motor, then spotted blue lights
coming toward them across the water. As the lights got closer, they realized
the source was a silver craft hovering just above the water's surface. The
craft was roughly 35 feet (10.7m) long, egg-shaped, and with a dome on
top, and it appeared to have windows on one side.

Before the men could run away, the craft hit them with a beam
that paralyzed them. Then three beings floated out of the craft and
glided above the water. Once these beings reached land, they walked
as stiffly as robots, but they looked like humanoids with reptilian skin.
No more than 5 feet (152cm) tall, they had large heads and large,
black eyes but only a slit where each one's mouth should be, and their
hands were like lobster claws. After they grabbed the men, Hickson
felt a sting on his shoulder before going into a trancelike state. Meanwhile, Parker passed out.

From this point, only Hickson could remember what happened. He reported that the beings took him and Parker into their craft and subjected them to a roughly 20-minute medical examination that involved photographing them and scanning them with a strange device. After this the beings returned Hickson and Parker to the pier before sending Hickson a telepathic message: "We are peaceful. We mean you no harm."[24] Parker regained consciousness just as the UFO was leaving.

Two Mississippi men who claimed to have encountered aliens while fishing on a river in 1973 described the beings as each having a large head, large black eyes, and a slit for a mouth. Investigators tried unsuccessfully to expose their account as a hoax.

Understandably upset by what they had just experienced, the two men rushed to a phone and called the nearest air force base, thinking the government would surely want to know about an alien invasion. But the base simply referred them to their local sheriff, Fred Diamond of Jackson County, Mississippi. Hickson and Parker went directly to his office, desperate to warn people about the aliens.

Examining Hickson and Parker

After hearing their tale, Diamond thought the men were pulling a prank. To see whether this was the case, he put the two men alone in a room with a concealed microphone. The sheriff thought that once they were by themselves, Hickson and Parker would begin to talk about how their hoax was going. Instead, their conversation made it clear that the two really believed they had experienced a frightening alien examination and that the aliens would soon be doing the same thing to other people.

> **DID YOU KNOW?**
>
> People who talk to aliens but are not abducted by them are called "contactees."

Diamond therefore concluded that the men were not pranksters—but because they had clearly been drinking, he suspected they might have just imagined the incident. To help rule this out, he took them to the doctor at the air force base to see if there was any physical evidence of their alien medical examination. The doctor found a small cut that suggested someone might have taken a blood sample from them, but otherwise they seemed untouched.

Still, both men remained consistent in repeating their story, and when air force intelligence officers gave Hickson a lie detector test, it showed that he believed he was telling the truth about what had happened inside the alien craft. In addition, after word of their experience got out, the men refused to profit from their experience, turning down a movie deal and leaving town to avoid the media. Parker also suffered from a nervous breakdown due to the stress of what he and Hickson had gone through.

In 2001, 28 years after this event took place, an officer in the US Navy came forward to claim that he too had seen an alien craft that night, in the same area hovering over a highway. This man, Naval Chief Petty Officer Mike Cataldo, insisted that he had reported the incident to several people in the military at the time it occurred. However, there appears to be no record of these reports, and skeptics note that a toll booth operator working near the pier that night did not see anything unusual.

Despite the lack of hard evidence of an alien abduction, many ufologists consider the Hickson-Parker encounter to be "one of the most important UFO cases in the 1970s," as William J. Birnes puts it in his book *Aliens in America*. Birnes notes that J. Allen Hynek, who was involved in a major government study on UFOs, investigated the case and concluded it was of an extraterrestrial nature. He adds, "This was quite an endorsement of the story's veracity by the nation's top skeptic, who later turned believer."[25]

> ## DID YOU KNOW?
>
> In his 2009 book, *Messages*, Stan Romanek says that after aliens abducted him, he was returned home wearing another abductee's shirt. He believes the aliens have trouble remembering trivial things like who was wearing which article of clothing.

Common Elements

In the years since the Hickson-Parker case, many other cases of alien abduction have surfaced. By the 1990s hundreds of people were calling themselves alien abductees, and reports of such encounters continue to surface. For example, a woman and her daughter in Aguada, Puerto Rico, recently reported having seen a disc-shaped UFO in a forest behind their house, first in November 2005 and then intermittently in 2006. One evening in April 2006, they claimed they saw two small Grey aliens in the woods, and after seeing them they felt drowsy. The next thing they knew, it was the next morning and they were in their beds. Later they

Food for Human-Alien Hybrids?

Some ufologists have theorized that aliens are responsible for cases of mysteriously mutilated livestock, because the mutilated bodies are sometimes cut so cleanly that it appears an advanced laser was involved. In fact, some researchers who have studied the sliced tissue say no device known on Earth could have made the cuts. By some estimates, over 10,000 such carcasses, particularly cattle, have been mutilated under mysterious circumstances, often with only the reproductive and digestive organs missing and little or no blood at the site.

Some ufologists have suggested these mutilations indicate that aliens are using livestock to test a virus that could be introduced into the human food chain, while others believe the aliens are gathering genetic material from the livestock, perhaps related to feeding the half-human, half-alien children—also known as alien-human hybrids—that abductees claim to have seen on alien spaceships. Indeed, some abductees have said that the hybrids look sickly, suggesting the aliens have not yet developed the means to nourish these half-humans properly. People who believe in government conspiracies have also insisted that the US military is somehow involved with the aliens' research, because mysterious black helicopters have occasionally been spotted in areas where mutilated cattle are later found. Skeptics, on the other hand, argue that only pranksters, members of a religious cult, or predators like coyotes can be to blame for the mutilations.

came to believe that they had been abducted and examined by aliens, even though they could not remember the event.

This inability to remember what happened during the abduction scenario is what ufologists call "missing time." Many people who believe they have been abducted by aliens say they have lost anywhere from an hour or two to a day or more. At the end of the episode, they often find themselves in an unexpected place with no memory of how they got there. If such memories surface later, it is typically through dreams or hypnosis.

When memories are retrieved, however, they are usually strikingly similar to abduction stories told by people who remember their experience immediately after the alien encounter. These stories follow a common sequence of events, typically including an alien medical examination. In addition, they share many details regarding what the aliens—usually Greys—and their ships look like.

Being Taken

The abduction story usually begins with the person encountering the alien while alone. In those few cases where the abductee is in a group, he or she reports that the aliens chose to abduct only one or two people from the group, leaving the rest behind in some kind of trance that ends when the abductees return. Ufologist and abduction researcher David M. Jacobs says: "Secrecy appears to be critically important to the aliens in determining the opportunities for abductions. . . . No abductions have surfaced that took place in the middle of a very large group of people, in full view of a public event."[26]

Often an abductee comes upon the aliens accidentally while in some remote place, but sometimes the abductee is drawn to that place through some inexplicable urge. For example, one abductee reported to Jacobs that once while driving late at night he felt compelled to travel a mile down a deserted road into a state park. He then stopped his car and walked into some woods, where he found a UFO. Other abductees have reported being taken while at home in bed, after aliens entered their rooms on a beam of light. Usually this light carried the aliens in through a window, open or closed, rather than through a wall or ceiling.

DID YOU KNOW?

Prominent abduction researcher Budd Hopkins was one of the first people to connect the phenomenon of missing time to alien abduction. His nonprofit organization, the Intruders Foundation, researches alien abductions and provides support to abductees.

Medical Examinations

In cases where the alien encounter has taken place at home, sometimes the aliens conduct a medical examination in the person's own room, but more often the aliens carry or float the person out of the house and into the spacecraft. Sometimes the person is conscious when this happens, but most often he or she is unaware of what is happening. As abductee Claire Chambers told abduction researcher Kenneth Ring:

> My boyfriend . . . and I were both removed from my bedroom in the night. My large dog attacked and injured one of the aliens. I fought also but was rendered unconscious. I awoke (in the craft I assume) in a strange environment lying on a table helpless with total paralysis. One alien was by my head and attempted to frighten me with his large eyes. The other aliens were working on my body. I was terrified and in great pain from the physical procedures they were doing to my body. At one point, I almost strangled and choked to death. I screamed, "NO! STOP! WHY?" over and over. There was no response from the alien lifeforms.[27]

No matter how the abductee arrives in the craft, many report having an experience similar to Chambers's while there. They typically say that the examination took place in a small, circular room with metallic floors and white and gray walls. Some abductees say that before the exam they spent time on a bench in a waiting room. Most also report that no part of their body was left unexamined and that aliens took skin, hair, blood, tissue, and sperm or ova samples. In addition, many abductees say that the aliens used odd machines to scan them. Abductee Tom Murillo's experience, as he reported it to Ring, is fairly typical:

> I was raised up into the spacecraft . . . where I landed on a glass-like table. I lay [there] for a few moments till these four tall aliens came into the room. They observed me for a while, then started their examination on me. A scanning device was used all the time. This device went around the glass table—above, sideways, under the table—and all the time I couldn't move a muscle except my eyes. All the data picked up by the scanning device was fed into a strange-shaped grey screen where I was fortunate to see my insides. My heart, my stomach, and other parts. I just lay there as I was examined.[28]

Implants and Tests

According to many abductees, at the end of the examination the aliens either place a small object inside their nose or ear or, if this is a repeat abduction, remove such an object. Some ufologists believe that this implant is similar to the tagging device that wildlife biologists on Earth use to track an animal for long-term study. Jacobs suggests it might also serve as a monitor of various human functions, such as hormone levels, or it might make it easier for the aliens to communicate with the person.

In addition, the device might be intended to make it easier for the aliens to abduct the same person again, because some abductees claim to have been taken several times. In such cases, typically the abductee reports seeing the same "boss alien" at every abduction, who seems to make note of any changes in the person's appearance. For example, one woman told Jacobs that the aliens took a sample of her gum tissue after they saw the braces on her teeth, apparently puzzled by the hardware in her mouth.

Some abductees also report being subjected to psychological tests. Some of these tests involve seeing images on a screen or in their minds that evoke a strong emotional response, either negative or positive, while an alien stares into the abductee's eyes to monitor his or her reactions. Other tests involve evaluating memory or pain thresholds. A few abductees have also claimed that aliens planted knowledge in their brains that they cannot remember; the recipients of this knowledge typically believe they will be able to recall it when it is needed in the future.

A few abductees report seeing half-alien, half-human children on board the spaceship as well. According to these abductees, the aliens

Alien Implant or Human Underwear?

Sometimes an abductee claims to have an alien implant, but none can be found. Other times an X-ray and/or physical examination reveal that a hard object is indeed under the person's skin. But to date, no doctor who has removed such an object has found it to be made of any material that does not exist on Earth. In fact, typically the object is discovered to be a piece of glass, metal, or wood that the body has surrounded with cells that became calcified, or hardened. This is the body's way of protecting itself from foreign "invaders."

In one of the most interesting cases in which this occurred, a scientist at the Massachusetts Institute of Technology, David Pritchard, discovered that one abductee's supposed implant was actually a fiber that had been encased with cells. Upon further examination, he realized this fiber had come from the abductee's underwear. In another case, however, the implant was discovered to be made of approximately a dozen minerals that, although they exist on Earth, are usually found together only in a meteor from outer space. Some ufologists therefore believe that this rock is an example of an alien implant, even though it has displayed no ability to transmit data to an alien spaceship.

encouraged them to hold and/or talk to the hybrids after explaining that a lack of human contact was making them sickly. In such cases abductees typically describe the children as extremely frail, with unusually thin bodies and very pale skin. The hybrids also have large eyes and large foreheads, but otherwise they typically appear more human than alien. Some repeat female abductees have reported feeling a kinship with a particular hybrid, leaving them to wonder whether the child was produced with one of the ova taken from them earlier. Abductees have also seen hybrid fetuses in incubator-like containers filled with fluid in alien laboratories.

Missing Memories

After the aliens are finished with them, most abductees are returned to the spot where their encounter began. A few, however, say that the aliens have mistakenly returned them to an unfamiliar spot. In either case the experience is said to have ended abruptly, and afterward most abductees cannot remember anything about what happened. Some believe this is because the aliens blocked the person's memory. Abductee and ufologist Budd Hopkins offers a possible reason for this:

> Memory blocks may . . . have to do with the abductee's role as a "human specimen" unwittingly being studied over a period of years. If people are being picked up as children, implanted with monitoring devices, and abducted a second time after puberty, at the very least the first abduction would have to be concealed. If the study is truly long range, the subjects would have to be kept in the dark about their role for many years, and a strongly effective block would have to be imposed.[29]

The Hill Case

In cases where memories have been blocked, abduction researchers typically use hypnosis to unblock them. According to some surveys, approximately 70 percent of people claiming to have been abducted by aliens remember their experience only through hypnosis. Ufologists have been using this procedure to retrieve abduction memories ever since the first widely reported case of alien abduction, that of Betty and Barney Hill in 1961.

On September 19 of that year, the Hills were driving home from Quebec, Canada, to Portsmouth, New Hampshire, when they saw an odd light in the night sky. Betty insisted it was a satellite, Barney an aircraft from a nearby air force base, and the 2 began arguing about which of them was right. They pulled over by the side of the road to look at the object with binoculars and realized that the craft was nothing human-

One of the most famous—and enduring—alien encounter stories involves Barney Hill (pictured) and his wife Betty. According to their story, the Hills were driving home from a trip to Canada in 1961 when the inhabitants of an alien spacecraft abducted them.

made. It was shaped like a pancake, ringed with windows through which shone an odd blue light, and had strange figures inside dressed in black uniforms. The Hills got the sense that the figures had seen them, and in a panic they jumped back in their car and sped away. The next thing they knew, they were 35 miles (56km) down the road, with no memory of having driven so far. Later they would realize that they were missing 3 hours out of their day; the trip from Canada to their home should have taken 4 hours, and instead it had taken 7.

A few days after this experience, Betty began having nightmares about being abducted and examined by aliens, while Barney began having panic attacks for which he sought psychiatric help. Soon Betty was convinced that they had had an alien encounter, especially given their missing time. For the next few years, she sought advice from ufologists and others about how to deal with this situation, while also speaking to gatherings of UFO enthusiasts.

In January 1964 the Hills finally underwent hypnosis in an attempt to retrieve their missing memories. Under hypnosis, Betty recalled events that were essentially the same as the ones in her nightmares, while Barney gave far more details as part of a more elaborate abduction story. Their hypnotist, Benjamin Simon, concluded that Barney's retrieved memories were actually a fantasy spurred by Betty's dreams and her fascination with UFOs. The Hills, however, stuck to their belief that they had been abducted by aliens. They cooperated with author John Fuller in presenting their story in his 1966 book *Interrupted Journey* and in a 1975 TV movie based on his book. These works, along with articles about the Hills, provided the public with what soon became a classic abduction scenario.

Media Exposure

Skeptics argue that the Hills are actually the reason this scenario is so common. The book and movie about the Hills were extremely popular, and Betty was a sought-after speaker in the UFO community. Consequently, many people were exposed to the details of her experience. Skeptics believe this is why so many abduction stories share the same details. Skeptics also point out that two weeks before the Hills were hypnotized, the TV series *The Outer Limits* aired an episode that featured aliens much like those the Hills described, suggesting that this was the source of the Hills' description of extraterrestrials.

However, the Hills' supporters believe there is hard evidence that the abduction really happened: a star map. While under hypnosis,

Betty recalled seeing this map on the aliens' ship, and after she re-created it, some experts in astronomy concluded that it represents a star system called Zeta Reticuli. Other experts disagree, arguing that Betty's "stars" are just random dots that form a pattern only somewhat similar to Zeta Reticuli.

Similar arguments rage in regard to abductees who claim to have physical evidence that proves they endured an alien medical exam. Marks said to be from alien incisions, scrapings, or needles might actually be ordinary scars, while supposed alien implants seem to be pieces of metal or other earthly objects. Consequently, skeptics like Philip Klass insist that "there is absolutely no scientifically credible physical evidence to indicate that the earth is being visited by extraterrestrials—let alone that they are abducting people."[30]

Alien Cleverness

But believers argue that this lack of evidence is due to the aliens' cleverness in concealing their activities. This would explain why aliens abduct people under circumstances that severely reduce the number of possible witnesses. It would also provide a reason for implants to look like ordinary metal. An unfamiliar material might alert the American public to alien efforts to tag and track humans. In this way, some ufologists argue, the aliens are behaving much like humans who study primitive cultures. Ufologist Johannes von Buttlar explains: "An open contact would disturb our society and its dynamics and influence it to such an extent that the results of the aliens' observations of it would be contaminated. Our anthropologists also try to keep to a minimum their influence on a society they wish to observe."[31]

Von Buttlar also suggests that the more unbelievable aspects of alien-encounter stories have been planted by aliens who want to make witnesses sound ridiculous "so that their reports do not find general acceptance and they are mostly regarded as fools or psychopaths."[32] Indeed, the scientific community and the press often ridicule people claiming to be abductees. Is this part of some alien plan? Even believers cannot agree on this, or on why extraterrestrials might be coming to Earth.

CHAPTER FOUR

Why Are People Encountering Aliens?

Certainly, some people reporting an alien encounter might be lying, perhaps for personal gain, or suffering from a mental illness that makes them imagine things that never occurred. But believers argue that given the large number of encounter reports, at least some of these experiences must have been real. If this is indeed the case, then where might these aliens be coming from and why?

Explorers or Researchers?

One of the most common theories is that the aliens are extraterrestrial astronauts similar to human astronauts, exploring planet Earth out of curiosity. Supporters of this theory say it explains why the aliens are so careful to land in remote areas, why they examine people and then return them unharmed, and why they do not leave behind any obvious evidence of their visits. Indeed, astronaut Edgar Mitchell, who once walked on the moon, says this is what he would have been instructed to do under similar circumstances. He explains that he and his crew would have "put [our spaceship] down in some very unpopulated region where we could examine the local fauna in safety and at our discretion. We would have wanted to pick up some living specimens, examine them, and put them back with a minimum of fuss, hoping to get back to Earth safely with as much information as possible."[33]

However, this theory does not account for the many abduction stories in which aliens are reported to have taken genetic material from humans and created human-alien hybrids. People who believe such stories theorize that instead of being nothing more than curious explorers, the aliens are scientists conducting some kind of research on humans, perhaps involving how genetics and/or environment affect human behavior. For example, ufologist Michael Mannion suggests that the aliens are studying humans to find out "what ails mankind"[34]—that is, why humans are so violent—and he believes the aliens might think the answer lies in how the fetus develops in the womb. Ufologist Budd Hopkins, on the other hand, suggests that the aliens might be "mining" genetic material or something just as valuable. Hopkins says, "We might indeed possess something—a natural resource, an element, a genetic structure—that an alien culture might desire to use, for example, as experimental raw material."[35]

Global Catastrophe

Others theorize that alien encounters have something to do with a future global catastrophe. Indeed, some abductees have said aliens told them telepathically that one day such a disaster will wipe out all humans and that human-alien hybrid children are being bred to repopulate the planet after that time. Similarly, abductee Betty Andreasson Luca believes aliens are studying people to determine how environmental pollution has been hurting humans and to come up with ways to repair this damage. Aliens are "the caretakers of nature and natural forms," she says. "They love mankind. They love the planet Earth and they have been caring for it and man since man's beginnings."[36]

Abductee George C. Andrews agrees that the aliens care about Earth, but he disagrees with the notion that they also care about human beings. He thinks they would be willing to destroy humankind in order to save the planet. In fact, he suspects that the aliens are coming to the planet because the spirit of Earth itself has called on them for help in ridding itself of humans. "Has Mother Earth asked to have her face cleaned?" he asks. "Have we been transforming our planet into a cancer cell in the body of the galaxy instead of making it the garden of the universe? Perhaps the

Christian, Islamic, Hebrew, Mazdean and Hopi traditions of Judgment Day refer to the day when the earth is once more 'relieved of its heavy load'"[37]—that is, relieved of all humans.

A similar theory is that the aliens are planning to kill all the humans on Earth and replace them with alien-human hybrids. This theory developed because abductees have said that the hybrids are weaker and more passive than humans; therefore, some people speculate that this passivity was intentionally bred into the hybrids. If so, then perhaps the hybrids are meant to serve as the aliens' slaves on Earth, or at least to provide Earth with humanlike caretakers that are not as violent and/or destructive to the environment as humans.

Time Travelers

But what if alien visitors to Earth are not aliens at all but humans traveling back in time from the future in hopes of preventing the human race from dying out? This is the thinking of some ufologists—that the devices that appear to be spacecraft are actually time machines, and that physical exams performed on abductees are part of studies ultimately intended to protect humanity. Believers in this idea say that confusion over the identity of these beings is understandable; the large heads and pale, frail bodies often described by those who have had encounters with them may look like extraterrestrial beings but are actually humans in an evolved physical state. Some scientists have even speculated that humans of the future will look like this if people continue to become more focused on indoor, intellectual activities, although no one knows for certain if time travel is really possible.

But while scientists disagree on whether time travel will ever be a reality, believers insist there is evidence that advanced humans are traveling

> ### DID YOU KNOW?
> Ufologists suspect that aliens are behind the creation of crop circles— intricate designs that appear in fields as if by magic—because no human has been able to duplicate 4,000 of the 10,000 such circles reported in 26 countries. Skeptics counter that pranksters must be to blame.

through time. Specifically, they point to unaltered photos that appear to show people in clothing and/or holding items too advanced for the time period. For example, in October 2010 someone noticed that within a screenshot of extra footage from a 1928 Charlie Chaplin film, a woman appears to be talking on a cell phone. Skeptics say these are cases of mistaken identity, where one thing simply looks like another in an old, usually grainy photo. But believers argue that no good reason exists to doubt such intriguing photographic evidence of time travel by people of the future.

Other Dimensions

Still another theory based on the idea that the "aliens" are not actually extraterrestrials relies on a belief in other dimensions. In this case what appear to be alien spaceships are instead portals linking two worlds, one in our dimension and another in an alternate dimension. This theory arose in large part because of discussions related to the connection between aliens and the phenomenon of crop circles.

Crop circles are intricate designs that appear as if by magic in fields of nearly ripe grain. The grain stalks within the designs have been swirled, bent, and flattened but not damaged, and many of the images demonstrate mathematical principles or represent ancient religious symbols. Since UFOs are often sighted right before the sudden appearance of these mysterious circles, some people have suggested that a hovering spaceship from another planet created the circle. However, many experts in crop circles say the phenomenon cannot be caused by spacecraft from another planet.

One such expert, Freddy Silva, explains why: "We can rule out crop circles as [spacecraft] landings [because accounts of such landings] . . . are generally associated with squashed plants, indentations, electronic

disruption, paralysis, burns, and harmful radioactivity."[38] Instead, Silva suggests, crop circles are caused by the manipulation of energy fields by a source within "a reality governed by rates of spin (some call it vibration) that differ from ours."[39] In other words, circle creation could require the kind of energy produced in another dimension, perhaps by a machine that we perceive as a UFO.

Silva also says that "when objects from other levels of reality alter their rate of spin they are observed as increasingly physical phenomena in our dimension."[40] In this way a being from another dimension would be able to alter matter, and the resulting physical phenomena might include crop circles. As for what kind of being might be able to accomplish this, Silva says it would have to possess "an understanding of the illusion of time, the function of gravity, knowledge of the proposed three speeds of light, and the spinning vortex action of molecules."[41] According to Silva, this being, which could be either a nonhuman or a highly evolved human, would require an advanced consciousness.

DID YOU KNOW?

Experts from the Search for Extraterrestrial Intelligence Institute are currently searching for radio and television signals from planetary systems within 80 light-years of Earth.

Similarly, some ufologists have suggested that the aliens, whether nonhuman or human, are coming from another universe linked to ours. In support of this idea, believers cite a theory among physicists that there are multiple interlocking universes, also known as multiverses or parallel universes, where more advanced humans live. What appear to be alien spacecraft, then, would be devices that enable intelligent beings to cross the divide between universes so they can study our world.

The Imaginal Realm

Another intriguing possibility suggested by some ufologists is that alien beings already live on Earth and that most people simply are not aware

The Near-Death Experience

Abduction stories typically bear a striking resemblance to reports of near-death experiences. A near-death experience occurs when doctors are able to revive someone who has just died and the person claims to have been able to hear and see things while dead. Many talk of having floated out of their bodies and traveled down a long tunnel with a bright light at the end of it, where one or more beings communicated with them telepathically. Sometimes near-death experiencers, or NDErs, also report having seen a vision of a global disaster that destroys Earth, and many subsequently express an interest in environmentalism. In addition, they usually come away from their experience with a greater appreciation for life and a heightened sense of spirituality.

Many abductees become more interested in spirituality after their experience as well, and they express the same feelings regarding environmentalism and the need to appreciate life. They also typically report having traveled—sometimes floating—down a tunnel to the alien spacecraft, toward a room with a bright light. Psychiatrist Kenneth Ring believes these commonalties between NDErs and abductees suggest both have experienced a higher level of consciousness. However, skeptics say that a near-death experience is just as much of a delusion as an abduction experience, and that the NDErs' visions happen not after death but during it, as the brain starts shutting down. Perhaps, such skeptics suggest, abduction memories are caused by a similar brain malfunction.

of them. Ufologists call these beings "ultraterrestrials" and suggest that it is by design that people usually do not recognize them. At times, however, they might allow people to see them for study purposes, or certain people—especially abductees—might have developed the ability to see ultraterrestrials whether or not these beings want to be seen.

Psychiatrist Kenneth Ring was among the first to suggest that abductees might have such an ability. He and others believe that when someone is seeing ultraterrestrials, he or she is accessing the imaginal realm, which Ring defines as a real place that is "the cumulative product of imaginative thought itself."[42] This realm has been connected to fairy tales, myths, and legends, whereby sightings of aliens are essentially the modern equivalent of sightings of creatures like goblins and trolls in earlier times.

In describing this realm, educator Mary Pat Mann says that if it existed it would be "a place outside of ordinary time and geography . . . where you had experiences, met people, did things in which you could participate but which you could not control. . . . [It] would feel real, and the experiences would affect you in real ways, even though you might maintain awareness that the reality was of a different order."[43] Descriptions of the so-called imaginal realm appear in so many myths, legends, and folk tales that it would appear to be real, says Mann. If it is, she believes, it can be accessed through trances, visualization, altered consciousness, religious rituals, and other heightened uses of imaginative powers. In other words, when people claim to have seen aliens, they might really have seen them, but only because their normal consciousness has been altered in a way that allows them to view the otherworldly.

The Collective Unconscious

Other explanations have been offered over the years for why people encounter—or think they encounter—alien species. The collective unconscious, first described by psychiatrist Carl Jung in the 1910s, has been cited as possibly playing a role in alien sightings. According to Jung, the collective unconscious is a part of the unconscious mind that stores ancient memories passed down from generation to generation. These memories are not exact recollections of real events; they rely on myths, symbols, and other imagery to pass on universal truths and deep-seated emotions.

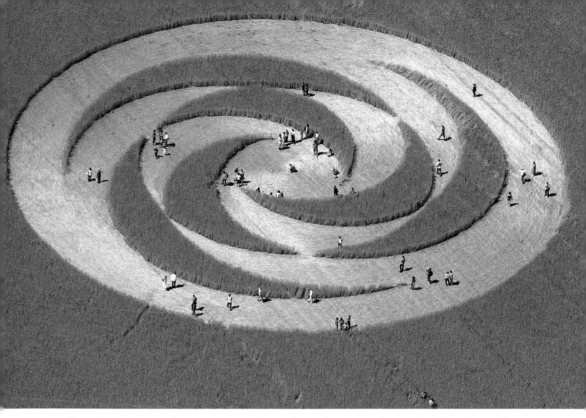

According to some theories, crop circles such as this one in Switzerland might result from the manipulation of energy fields by beings from other dimensions. These beings would have to be highly evolved and possess an advanced state of consciousness.

In other words, stories of alien encounters might be the result of dreams or nightmares that have drawn on images from the collective unconscious. Supporters of this theory note that most encounter stories take place at night, when people could have dozed off, and that most abduction stories begin and end with the person in a dreamlike state. And like those who believe in the imaginal realm theory, believers in the collective unconscious theory point out that the aliens bear similarities to creatures that have been part of folklore and mythology for generations.

Peter Brookesmith, an expert in UFO sightings, believes that the connection between stories of aliens and stories of elves, goblins, and similar beings proves that "the human mind is inextricably involved with all UFO phenomena, from 'simple' sightings of flying disks to complex, full-blown abduction accounts."[44] Others, however, suggest that the key to understanding alien encounters lies not in fairy tales and mythology but in spirituality and mysticism. In the opinion of these people the journey to the spaceship and back again is essentially a spiritual journey that leads to permanent changes in the way a person views the world, and any fear or pain associated with this journey is caused not by an actual alien abduction or medical examination but by the mind's reaction to expanding its awareness. In other words, alien encounters are actually a type of spiritual journey.

Brain Activity

Indeed, scientists and psychologists have noted similarities between people who have reported alien encounters and those who have had mystical or visionary experiences. Both types of people typically say that the world is full of mysteries, that many of these mysteries will probably never be solved, and that things are not always as they seem. Both types also tend to exhibit electrical surges in the temporal lobes of the brain, which are involved with accessing memories and processing perceptions related to sound, vision, and speech.

> **DID YOU KNOW?**
>
> Scientist and ufologist Jacques Vallée, who served as the model for French researcher Claude Lacombe in Steven Spielberg's movie on alien encounters, *Close Encounters of the Third Kind,* is a leading proponent of the theory that the aliens come from another dimension outside of space and time.

In the 1980s neuroscientist Michael Persinger began conducting experiments to determine what people might be experiencing when such electrical surges occur. Using fluctuating magnetic fields in order to trigger surges in the cerebral cortex, where the temporal lobes are located, he hoped to cause and/or influence a variety of paranormal and/or spiritual experiences in his test subjects. Based on their reports, Persinger says he has been able to re-create nearly every known paranormal, spiritual, and religious experience, including alien encounters, through electrical stimulation. However, other researchers' attempts to duplicate his results, which began in late 2004, have so far been unsuccessful.

Still, even Persinger's critics admit that another of his discoveries is correct: that reports of UFO sightings, alien abductions, and religious visions increase during times of great seismic activity, when there are changes in Earth's magnetic field. Many people believe that this finding supports the notion that changes in the brain might be causing alien encounters. Critics of this theory, however, correctly note that not all alien encounters happen around the time of an earthquake, and not all abductees experience electrical surges in the brain.

Far more common is a connection between alien encounters and childhood traumas. That is, individuals who were abused as children, whether by strangers or family members, are far more likely to report being abused by aliens. Consequently, some ufologists believe that extraterrestrials are more likely to select as victims those people who have been traumatized—either because they are less likely to fight back or because their psychological makeup is something the aliens want to study and/or are drawn to. Psychiatrists, however, suggest that alien abduction stories are actually disguised memories of childhood abuse, with the aliens as stand-ins for abusive family members.

Some psychiatrists believe that what abductees are remembering is not childhood abuse but their own birth. The birth-trauma theory suggests that the human mind can take the deep memory of a person's passage from the dark womb down the birth canal to a brightly lit delivery room and turn it into a story of being transported from dark woods into a spaceship within which a tunnel typically leads to a brightly lit examining room. And just as newborns experience painful procedures they do not understand, so too do abductees.

False Memories

But skeptics say that another kind of memory can be responsible for reports of alien encounters: the false memory. False memories can develop when someone under hypnosis says things the hypnotist wants to hear. This is most likely to occur when the hypnotized person is eager to please and the hypnotist asks leading questions that encourage certain types of answers.

Abduction researcher David M. Jacobs insists that "most abductees refuse to be led"[45] to say things that are not true while under hypnosis, but skeptics say it is impossible to know whether this is the case. Skeptics also point out that under certain circumstances, most children and many adults will make up stories when asked to talk about things they know nothing about. Likewise, eyewitnesses to crimes will sometimes invent details in order to be more "helpful" to police. At first the storyteller might be aware that he or she is making things up, but over time, the person comes to believe that what he or she said was the truth.

Tales of mystical beings such as elves, pictured (opposite) dancing in a circle in the painting The Elf Ring, have been around for centuries. Such tales, one expert says, might influence the human mind and explain some of the sightings of mysterious beings from other worlds.

Government Involvement

But what if stories about alien encounters are being created not by the storytellers or their hypnotists but by agents of the US government? Some people have suggested that such agents are producing alien-related hallucinations, via experimental drugs, in certain people as part of mind-control experiments. Others think these hallucinations are being produced in order to make abductees look like disturbed people who cannot be believed, thereby discrediting the notion that extraterrestrials are actually coming to Earth. Under this theory, stories of alien abduction induced in test subjects are part of ongoing government attempts to hide the truth about extraterrestrials—attempts that began with the weather balloon story that surfaced right after the Roswell crash.

Supporters of this and other government conspiracy theories argue that the US government has not conducted serious research into alien encounters specifically because it does not want the public to take the subject seriously. Indeed, even some people who do not believe in such conspiracies wonder why the government has not supported serious scientific studies into UFO-related phenomena. Instead, those who express an interest in studying extraterrestrials are often ridiculed.

Scientific Study

It is not just the government that has failed to take alien-encounter reports seriously; many researchers and investigators are guilty of this as well. As Thomas E. Bullard explains in his book *The Myth and Mystery of UFOs*:

> Though popular with the public and a staple image in everyday life, [reports of UFO and alien sightings] cannot even get off the ground as a matter of interest among the scientists and journalists who ought to lead the way in exploring the matter. Thousands of people have UFO experiences every year but seldom find anyone willing to listen, any acknowledgment that the objects of their puzzlement count as anything more than trivial entertainment or intellectual junk.[46]

Believers correctly note, however, that such hasty dismissals have been proved wrong in the past. For example, in the book *The Abduction Enigma*, the authors report:

> Science rejected rocks from the sky (meteorites) until a proper scientific study was completed in France that proved rocks could fall from the sky. Science scoffed at the idea of a living fossil, rejecting reports that a coelacanth had been captured in a fisherman's net. But it was science, when presented with the proper evidence, that reversed itself, amazed that the fish had survived its alleged extinction seventy-five million years earlier.[47]

Consequently, ufologists argue that one day, scientific studies might reveal not only that alien encounters are real experiences but why these experiences are occurring. But first the media and the scientific community as a whole must take reports of alien encounters seriously. Otherwise questions about alien encounters will go unanswered, and various, often conflicting theories related to such experiences will continue to be proposed.

SOURCE NOTES

Introduction: Fiction or Fact?

1. Jim Marrs, *Alien Agenda: Investigating the Extraterrestrial Presence Among Us*. New York: HarperCollins, 1997, p. xi.

Chapter One: Seeing Dead Aliens

2. Quoted in Kevin D. Randle and Donald R. Schmitt, *UFO Crash at Roswell*. New York: Avon, 1991, p. 54.
3. Randle and Schmitt, *UFO Crash at Roswell*, p. 54.
4. Quoted in Randle and Schmitt, *UFO Crash at Roswell*, p. 143.
5. Randle and Schmitt, *UFO Crash at Roswell*, p. 7.
6. Timothy Printy, "Alien Autopsies," *Roswell 4F: Fabrications, Fumbled Facts, and Fables*. Self-published e-book, 1997–1999. http://home.comcast.net/~tprinty/UFO/Dennis.htm.
7. Thomas E. Bullard, *The Myth and Mystery of UFOs*. Lawrence: University Press of Kansas, 2010, p. 81.
8. National Library of Australia, *UFO Crash at Roswell: The Genesis of a Modern Myth*, catalogue summary. http://catalogue.nla.gov.au.
9. Robert T. Carroll, "Roswell," *The Skeptic's Dictionary*, December 9, 2010. www.skeptic.com.
10. Carroll, "Roswell."
11. Quoted in "UFO Claim over Wind Farm Damage," BBC News, January 8, 2009. http://news.bbc.co.uk.

Chapter Two: Seeing Live Aliens

12. Quoted in "The Metal Man of Falkville (Alabama, USA)," American Monsters, March 3, 2010. http://americanmonsters.com.
13. Quoted in "The Metal Man of Falkville (Alabama, USA)."

14. William J. Birnes, *Aliens in America: A UFO Hunter's Guide to Extraterrestrial Hotspots Across the US*. Avon, MA: Adams Media, 2010, p. 89.

15. Birnes, *Aliens in America*, p. 91

16. Birnes, *Aliens in America*, pp. 91–92.

17. Cherry Hinkle, "Reptilian Encounter in the Nevada Desert," *UFO Digest*, November 11, 2010. www.ufodigest.com.

18. Donald Worley, "Nordic Alien Type Experiences," Alien Abduction Experience and Research, 1996–2011. www.abduct.com.

19. Quoted in Worley, "Nordic Alien Type Experiences."

20. Jim Moroney, *The Extraterrestrial Answer Book: UFOs, Alien Abductions, and the Coming ET Presence*. Charlottesville, VA: Hampton Roads, 2009, p. 57.

21. Aaron Sakulich, "'Gray' Aliens Product of Past Popular Imagination," *Triangle*, May 20, 2005. www.thetriangle.org.

22. Sakulich, "'Gray' Aliens Product of Past Popular Imagination."

23. Sakulich, "'Gray' Aliens Product of Past Popular Imagination."

Chapter Three: Abducted by Aliens

24. Rupert Matthews, *Alien Encounters: True-Life Stories of Aliens, UFOs, and Other Extra-Terrestrial Phenomena*. Edison, NJ: Chartwell, 2008, p. 165.

25. Birnes, *Aliens in America*, p. 131.

26. David M. Jacobs, *Secret Life: Firsthand Documented Accounts of UFO Abductions*. New York: Simon & Schuster, 1992, p. 50.

27. Quoted in Kenneth Ring, *The Omega Project: Near-Death Experiences, UFO Encounters, and Mind at Large*. New York: William Morrow, 1992, p. 79.

28. Quoted in Kenneth Ring, *The Omega Project*, p. 82.

29. Budd Hopkins, *Missing Time*. New York: Ballantine, 1981, p. 223.

30. Philip Klass, *UFO Abductions*. New York: Prometheus, 1989, p. 6.

31. Quoted in Michael Hesemann, *UFOs: The Secret History*. New York: Marlowe, 1998, p. xiv.

32. Quoted in Hesemann, *UFOs*, p. xiv.

Chapter Four: Why Are People Encountering Aliens?

33. Quoted in Hopkins, *Missing Time*, p. 16.
34. Michael Mannion, *Project Mindshift: The Re-Education of the American Public Concerning Extraterrestrial Life, 1947–Present*. New York: M. Evans, 1998, p. 293.
35. Hopkins, *Missing Time*, p. 212.
36. Quoted in Raymond Fowler, *The Watchers: The Secret Design Behind UFO Abduction*. New York: Bantam, 1990, p. 202.
37. George C. Andrews, *Extra-Terrestrials Among Us*. St. Paul, MN: Llewellyn, 1986, p. 291.
38. Freddy Silva, *Secrets in the Fields: The Science and the Mysticism of Crop Circles*. Charlottesville, VA: Hampton Roads, 2002, p. 145.
39. Silva, *Secrets in the Fields*, p. 144.
40. Silva, *Secrets in the Fields*, p. 144.
41. Silva, *Secrets in the Fields*, p. 144.
42. Ring, *The Omega Project*, p. 219.
43. Mary Pat Mann, "The Door to the Imaginal Realm," *Mytholog*, Summer 2006. www.mytholog.com.
44. Peter Brookesmith, *UFO: The Complete Sightings*. New York: Barnes & Noble, 1995, p. 8.
45. Jacobs, *Secret Life*, p. 291.
46. Bullard, *The Myth and Mystery of UFOs*, pp. 7–8.
47. Kevin D. Randle, Russ Estes, and William P. Cone, *The Abduction Enigma*. New York: Tom Doherty, 1999, p. 363.

FOR FURTHER EXPLORATION

Books

William J. Birnes, *Aliens in America: A UFO Hunter's Guide to Extraterrestrial Hotspots Across the US*. Avon, MA: Adams Media, 2010. This book offers a guide to places across the United States that have become famous for UFO sightings and alien encounters.

Thomas E. Bullard, *The Myth and Mystery of UFOs*. Lawrence: University Press of Kansas, 2010. For more advanced readers, this book offers detailed information about various UFO-related theories.

Jerome Clark, *Hidden Realms, Lost Civilizations, and Beings from Other Worlds*. Canton, MI: Visible Ink, 2010. Written by an expert in the paranormal, this book includes information on UFOs and extraterrestrials as well as other paranormal topics.

Preston Dennett, *UFOs and Aliens*. New York: Checkmark, 2008. This book for young adults provides interesting information about UFOs and extraterrestrials.

John G. Fuller, *The Interrupted Journey: Two Lost Hours "Aboard a Flying Saucer."* New York: Dial, 1966. This was the first major work on alien abduction, publicizing the phenomenon by documenting the case of Betty and Barney Hill.

David M. Jacobs, *Secret Life: Firsthand Documented Accounts of UFO Abductions*. New York: Simon & Schuster, 1992. For more advanced readers, this provides interesting firsthand accounts of alien abduction.

Philip Klass, *Bringing UFOs Down to Earth*. New York: Prometheus, 1997. Written by a leading skeptic, this book for young readers provides guidelines for thinking critically about UFOs.

Rupert Matthews, *Alien Encounters: True-Life Stories of Aliens, UFOs, and Other Extra-Terrestrial Phenomena*. Edison, NJ: Chartwell, 2008. Matthews provides many interesting stories of UFO sightings and alien encounters, including classic cases.

Jim Moroney, *The Extraterrestrial Answer Book: UFOs, Alien Abductions, and the Coming ET Presence*. Charlottesville, VA: Hampton Roads, 2009. For more advanced readers, Moroney presents his own theories on what might be the reason for alien encounters.

Kevin D. Randle, *Crash: When UFOs Fall from the Sky; A History of Famous Incidents, Conspiracies, and Cover-Ups*. Pompton Plains, NJ: Career, 2010. Written by a ufologist, this book provides details about some of the most famous events in UFO history.

Stan Romanek, *Messages: The World's Most Documented Extraterrestrial Contact Story*. Woodbury, MN: Llewellyn, 2009. For more advanced readers, this work provides details about Romanek's experiences as an alien abductee.

Chris A. Rutkowski, *The Big Book of UFOs*. Ontario: Dundurn, 2010. This book provides details about many UFO cases as well as offering trivia and other information related to the subject.

Websites

American Monsters (http://americanmonsters.com). This site provides information on a wide variety of "monster" sightings, including ones involving monsters suspected of being extraterrestrials.

"The Crop Circles Phenomenon: A Beginners Guide," *Swirled News* (www.swirlednews.com/crop.asp). This website provides a wealth of information about crop circles.

"ETs and UFOs," *The Skeptic's Dictionary* (www.skepdic.com/tialien.html). This section of *The Skeptic's Dictionary* provides a skeptic's view of subjects related to alien encounters.

Skeptical Inquirer (www.csicop.org). This website has an archive of articles by skeptics regarding a variety of topics related to the paranormal.

UFO Casebook (www.ufocasebook.com). This website offers numerous articles about topics related to UFOs.

UFO Digest (www.ufodigest.com). The *UFO Digest* website reports on UFO, alien, and paranormal experiences around the world.

UFO Evidence (www.ufoevidence.org). This website provides articles about a variety of topics related to UFOs and extraterrestrials.

"UFO Files," *Fortean Times* (www.forteantimes.com/strangedays/ufo-files). This section of the *Fortean Times* website offers information on current and past alien encounters.

"UFOs and Aliens," **About.com** (http://ufos.about.com). The About.com website includes a section on UFOs and aliens that provides interesting information about both classic and recent alien encounters.

INDEX

Note: Boldface page numbers indicate illustrations.

mass hysteria explanation, 25–26
media influence, 9, 37–38
physical evidence and, 22–23, 43
Roswell incident
    changes in story, 21
    delusions and establishment of
        Roswell memory, 21–22
    differing descriptions of aliens, 14
    of Haut, 10
    logical explanation of physical
        evidence, 12
    mixing memories, 18
    similarity to myths, 21
Spencer photograph, 8
Skeptic's Dictionary, The (Carroll),
    21–22
Spencer, Philip, 6–8, **7**
Spielberg, Steven, 62
star map of Zeta Reticuli, 50–51
Sutton family, 31–32

technology, as reason for government
    cover-ups, 20
theories
    aliens and global catastrophe, 54–55
    aliens as astronauts, 53–54
    aliens as from different dimension,
        56, 58, 61, 62
    aliens as scientists, 53
    aliens as time travelers, 55–56, 57
    aliens as ultraterresterials on Earth,
        58–60
    aliens from other universes, 58
    brain activity similarities, 62–63
    childhood trauma, 63–64

collective unconscious, 60–61
fairy tales and myths, 61–62, 65
government conspiracies, 66
Tibet-China border, bodies discovered,
    15
time travelers, aliens as, 55–56, **57**

UFO Crash at Roswell (Randle and
    Schmitt), 15, 17
*UFO Crash at Roswell: The Genesis of
    a Modern Myth* (Saler, Ziegler, and
    Moore), 21
ufologists, 8
UFOs, number of Americans who
    claim sighting of, 8
ultraterresterials on Earth, aliens as,
    58–60

Vallée, Jacques, 62
Venus, aliens from, 37
videotape by Cornet, 36
von Buttlar, Johannes, 51–52

Walter Reed Hospital, 20
"War of the Worlds, The" (H.G.
    Wells), 32
water, attraction to, 30, 31
weather balloons, as source of Roswell
    materials, 13
Wells, H.G., 32, 37
Wells, Orson, 32
Worley, Donald, 33

Zeta Reticuli, 51
Ziegler, Charles A., 21

PICTURE CREDITS

ABOUT THE AUTHOR

Patricia D. Netzley is the author of dozens of books for children, teens, and adults. Her works include *Alien Abductions* (Lucent Books, 2001), *UFOs* (Lucent Books, 2000), and *The Greenhaven Encyclopedia of Paranormal Phenomena* (Greenhaven Press, 2006). She lives in Southern California with her three children—Matthew, Sarah, and Jacob—and her husband Raymond.